MODERN JAIL LEADERSHIP

BUILDING HEALTHY, RESILIENT, AND COMPLIANT INSTITUTIONS

Crayman J. Harvey

Copyright © 2026 Crayman J. Harvey

All rights reserved.

No part of this publication may be reproduced, distributed, or transmitted in any form or by any means, including photocopying, recording, or other electronic or mechanical methods, without the prior written permission of the publisher, except in the case of brief quotations embodied in critical reviews and certain other non-commercial uses permitted by copyright law.

ISBN: 9798218784614

Edit and Layout by Shonell Bacon
Book Publishing Coach: Telishia Berry, StriveIPG.com

Dedication

To my family, thank you for your unwavering support, patience, and understanding. For every late night, missed holiday, school event, or quiet moment interrupted by a call or crisis, please know that your sacrifice made a difference. You allowed me to serve, to lead, and to carry out a mission I believe in with all my heart. This work hasn't always been easy, but because of you, it's always been worth it.

With love and gratitude,

Crayman

Contents

	Acknowledgments	i
	Foreword	1
	Introduction	5
1	The Evolution of Jail Leadership	8
2	Defining a Healthy Jail: Beyond Compliance to Culture	16
3	Building Culture Through Leadership	27
4	Leading Through Crisis and Change	40
5	Balancing Security, Health, and Rehabilitation	53
6	Hiring, Training, and Developing People	63
7	Sustaining Culture Through Accountability and Consistency	76
8	Leadership Beyond the Walls: Professionalism, Community, and the Future	89
	References & Resources	101
	About the Author	103

Acknowledgments

No book, and no journey, in leadership is ever walked alone.

First and foremost, I want to thank **God**, who gave me the strength, clarity, and conviction to lead even in the most challenging seasons.

To my **family**, your patience, sacrifices, and unwavering belief in me gave me the freedom to serve others, often at the expense of time with you. Every missed moment was felt, and every moment of grace you gave me will never be forgotten.

To the **teams I've had the privilege to lead**, in times of calm and in crisis, thank you for your dedication to the mission. You taught me as much as I ever taught you.

To the mentors and professionals who challenged and encouraged me, especially **Dr. John Thompson**, thank you for provoking me to grow, lead with purpose, and continue coaching others to do the same.

To all correctional officers, supervisors, administrators, and behind-the-scenes professionals who wake up each day to serve in this difficult profession, this book is for you. May it remind you that your leadership matters, your culture matters, and your people matter.

And finally, to the next generation of correctional leaders: take the torch, raise the standard, and never forget—**the culture you allow is the culture you lead.**

Foreword

Modern Jail Leadership: Building Healthy, Resilient, and Compliant Institutions is a valuable book for leaders, managers, and front line staff members who desire to take jail management to the next level that yields highly engaged and productive professionals committed to excellence. The next level calls for a culture change that results in a win-win situation for both staff and detainees. I applaud Crayman Harvey for investing the time to succinctly capture both the high and low points of leadership practices that he experienced in his over two decades of service in jail administration. This book is a distillation of practical approaches that shape a healthy work culture fueled by committed team players.

In reading this book and reflecting on your own experiences working in a jail, you will discover that the old way of doing business is ineffective and counterintuitive in the current day and time. That old way of leading as an authoritarian with a heavy fist, instilling fear, lack of a genuine connection with staff, and/or no support of staff leads to a failed jail system full of disgruntled and burned-out staff members. Unfortunately, these very staff members continue to put their lives on the line to serve and protect the lives and safety of detainees who are awaiting trial and, for some, facing lengthy prison sentences. The irony of protecting the lives of others is that the guards face great danger themselves when some detainees do not regard the wellbeing of humanity. Thus, it is commonplace for detainees to inflict harm when things do not go their way.

These factors are a recipe for hostile work environments consisting of a disengaged workforce collecting a paycheck with no passion or commitment for the work. Moreover, these staff members are led by a command staff who is disconnected from the line staff's world. In other words, some leaders and managers lack the proper skills and ability to effect positive change in the organization. Yes, the very leaders and managers may know policy, regulations, and law; however, they lack emotional intelligence and interpersonal skills and the ability to influence those reporting to them. Gone are the days that simply paying someone should be adequate for them to come to work, be happy, and do a great job. Welcome to a new day with a generation that has a different perspective about life and public service let alone working in a jail.

Thus, reading this book will help you to recalibrate the way that you run your jail. You will gain tangible insights based on theory and practical application of how to develop and sustain an engaged workforce that is passionate about public service. As you adopt the theories Mr. Harvey delivers in this book, you will begin to see a jail workforce that is committed to excellence. After reading *Modern Jail Leadership*, you will inspire your team to greatness by empowering them on every shift and in every job.

John M. Thompson, Ph.D., ICMA-CM, CPM

INTRODUCTION

There was a time when I thought leadership in corrections meant having all the answers, giving all the orders, and keeping the chaos at bay. I quickly learned that this wasn't leadership at all. True leadership in a jail setting is about trust between staff, between leadership and the front line, and between the institution and the community it serves. It's about setting a tone where people feel valued, heard, and supported, even in one of the most challenging environments you can imagine. After more than two decades leading adult and juvenile detention facilities, I've come to believe this: The culture inside a jail reflects the character of its leadership. This book is my attempt to help today's correctional leaders—and those stepping into this difficult role—build healthy, resilient, and compliant institutions where people can thrive, not just survive.

Out of pain, mistakes, lessons learned, and many moments of reflection, I felt compelled to write this book to turn my past experiences into a practical guide for other leaders. My hope is that this serves as a reference to help navigate the challenges of jail operations that test not only your leadership skills, but also your mental toughness and emotional resilience.

My leadership journey did not begin as a facility administrator or agency director. It began as a frontline correctional officer, a 23-year-old who had just returned from working overseas for a subcontractor. At the time, I was simply eager to find steady work. I didn't expect to build a career in corrections, but one opportunity led to another. I found myself working 12-hour night shifts (and often more), passing meals, medication, laundry, and other necessities to men and women—some much older than me—in close quarters where violence, misconduct, and moral challenges were ever-present. In those long shifts, in that difficult environment, my leadership journey truly began.

More than 20 years later, that young man has advanced through the ranks, from managing state juvenile facilities and small and large adult jails, to serving as an educator, and now launching my own consulting firm. This advancement is not because I claim to be the smartest in policies, procedures, or advanced education—but because I was fortunate enough to learn from great mentors, to listen, and to follow wise leadership.

Today, more than ever, correctional leadership is critical. Leaders are the culture of their organizations, —and culture drives outcomes, not just compliance.

It is my hope that this book will serve as a mirror, not just a checklist, helping correctional leaders at all levels reflect, grow, and strengthen themselves for the benefit of their staff, the people in their care, and their own professional journey.

Chapter 1

THE EVOLUTION OF JAIL LEADERSHIP

The Old Model: Rank, Command, and Control

There was a time when leadership in jails and detention facilities was defined almost entirely by rank and command. The one with the badge, the title, and the power set the tone—and that tone was often one of control, authority, and compliance through force of will. In my early days working the night shift as a young correctional officer, I saw this style play out daily. Orders were given, orders were followed—and too often, staff and inmates alike operated in an environment shaped by fear and exhaustion, not trust or professionalism. At that time, I thought that was simply the nature of the job.

Modern Jail Leadership

Learning Through Observation: What Was Missing

But over the years, through hard-earned lessons, crises, and mentorship from leaders I deeply respected, I came to realize that effective leadership in this field is about much more. It's about the culture you create as a leader. It's about building trust at every level of the organization. And it's about understanding that the health of a jail is not measured only by incident reports or audits, but by the day-to-day human experience inside those walls, for staff and detainees alike. This evolution in leadership mindset didn't come overnight for me, and in many ways, I am still learning and growing. What follows in this chapter is my reflection on that journey and the lessons I hope will serve today's and tomorrow's correctional leaders.

My earliest image of a jail leader was shaped by watching a tall, professionally dressed woman who served as the facility administrator. She arrived at the facility, entered her office, and remained behind closed doors for most of her shift—except during mandatory monthly training. After those sessions, she would occasionally ask staff if they had suggestions to improve the facility. Coming from a military background, this style of leadership felt very different to me. I was used to leaders who were visible, directive, and always engaged. Here, I was expected to be self-sufficient, but something felt missing.

Later, I worked under a second director, one much more involved in day-to-day operations. This leader closely monitored the cameras, watched activity on computer screens, and routinely called managers to address minor issues throughout the day. On the surface, it seemed like they had complete control, and managers appeared responsive, but again, something was missing.

The Hidden Cost of Poor Leadership

Both leadership styles, one detached and one overly controlling, had negative impacts on morale, staff relationships, and ultimately, the culture of the organization. Yes, they both exercised control, but neither built meaningful connections with staff or detainees. Both failed to foster an environment where trust, professionalism, and shared purpose could take root. Over time, their leadership approaches contributed to cultures of fear and authoritarianism, rather than engagement and respect.

My Leadership Evolution

My personal leadership evolution has not been a straight path. Like many in this profession, I began as a frontline correctional officer, a young man returning from overseas contract work, simply looking for an opportunity. At that point, I didn't see myself as a "leader." I saw myself as someone doing the job:

working long shifts, following orders, passing out meals, managing housing units. I relied on what I had learned from my military background and from watching the supervisors around me. In those early years, I believed leadership was about rank, giving orders, and making sure things got done.

As I moved up through the ranks—classification officer, lieutenant, then manager—my leadership style was still very much command-driven. I could tell people what to do. I could correct their behavior. I could enforce policies. But what I began to notice was this: control alone didn't build strong teams. The same staff who followed orders would sometimes disengage, burn out, or leave. Morale was fragile. I started asking myself, *What kind of leader would I want to follow?*

Fortunately, I had the opportunity to work under mentors who modeled something different. They led with trust. They listened more than they talked. They gave staff ownership in solving problems. And they were visible, not locked in an office or only reacting to crises. The more I observed this style of leadership, the more I realized that leadership wasn't about compliance; it was about connection. The stronger the connection between leadership and staff, the stronger the organization became.

Over the years, I carried these lessons with me as I transitioned into executive leadership, managing both juvenile and adult detention facilities, leading culture change efforts, and eventually launching Harvey

Consulting. Today, my view of leadership continues to evolve. Leadership is not about knowing it all. It's about staying humble, building trust, and creating cultures where people want to come to work and do their best because they believe in the mission.

The Changing Role of Jail Leadership

The role of a jail leader today is far more complex than it was even a decade ago. The expectations placed on leadership have evolved rapidly, shaped by legal mandates, public accountability, workforce challenges, and the growing understanding of human needs inside correctional environments. Gone are the days when a facility director or warden could focus solely on maintaining order and controlling movement. Today's leaders must also be stewards of wellness, culture, and organizational integrity.

The Rise of Professional Standards

One major driver of this shift has been the widespread adoption of professional standards: ACA accreditation, NCCHC healthcare standards, and PREA requirements for protecting against sexual assault in custody. These frameworks push facilities toward measurable outcomes: providing adequate health care, protecting vulnerable populations, training staff on human rights obligations, and ensuring leadership accountability. But these standards alone do not create culture. That still falls to leadership. If leaders treat these mandates as "check-the-box" exercises, staff will do the same. If leaders embrace them as tools for improving safety, dignity, and morale, the entire facility benefits.

Mental Health, Trauma, and Wellness: A Leadership Responsibility

Equally important is the growing recognition of how mental health, trauma, and wellness affect everyone in the facility, staff as well as inmates. Today's leaders must understand that correctional officers working long shifts in high-stress environments are at risk of burnout, depression, and secondary trauma. And those in custody often bring extensive histories of trauma, substance use, and mental illness. Leadership that ignores these realities creates brittle, reactive organizations. Leadership that acknowledges and addresses them through wellness initiatives, training, and modeling emotional intelligence creates facilities that can weather stress and change.

The Demand for Emotional Intelligence and Trust

Finally, legal and societal expectations have shifted dramatically. Lawsuits, public inquiries, and investigative journalism now hold jail leadership more accountable than ever. The community rightly expects transparency and ethical governance. Trust, communication, and integrity are now non-negotiable leadership qualities. Emotional intelligence is no longer optional. It is essential. The modern correctional leader must be skilled in listening, coaching, conflict resolution, and relationship-building not just compliance and command.

Leading with Purpose and Humanity

As I learned through my own evolution, and through watching great mentors, the most effective leaders today lead with purpose and humanity. As John Maxwell says, "Leadership is not about titles, positions, or flowcharts. It is about one life influencing another." That truth applies to every level of correctional leadership.

Chapter Reflection

As I continue this leadership journey, one truth remains constant: leadership defines the culture of any facility. Policies matter. Standards matter, but it is the tone set by leadership through words, actions, and values that ultimately shapes whether a jail becomes a healthy, resilient institution or one that struggles with dysfunction. My hope is that the lessons shared in this book will inspire correctional leaders to reflect on their own approach and to lead with greater purpose, trust, and humanity. Because in this profession, leadership is not a title; it is a daily choice.

Reflection Questions

1. How would your staff describe the culture of your facility, and how is your leadership influencing that culture?
2. What small changes could you make this month to lead with greater trust, transparency, and emotional intelligence?

Chapter 2

DEFINING A HEALTHY JAIL: BEYOND COMPLIANCE TO CULTURE

"The culture of any organization is shaped by the worst behavior the leader is willing to tolerate."
Gruenter & Whitaker

"You cannot inspect culture into a facility—you have to lead it."
Crayman J. Harvey

What makes a jail "healthy"? For years, many would have answered with statistics: low incidents of violence, passing audits, minimal grievances. No headlines from local reporters. The public barely noticing the jail, as if it's not part of the community it serves.

But I've come to believe that a truly healthy jail is measured by far more than numbers on a report. It is reflected in the morale of the staff, the professionalism of day-to-day interactions, the respect shown toward those in custody, and the level of trust between leadership and the team. A healthy jail fosters resilience in both its workforce and its culture.

And in today's environment, where staffing challenges, mental health needs, and public scrutiny are greater than ever, jail leaders must move beyond compliance alone. They must actively build the type of culture where people can do their best work, and where dignity and safety are prioritized for all.

The Leadership Lens: How Culture Impacts Health

As Peter Drucker famously said, "Culture eats strategy for breakfast." In corrections, culture also eats policy, procedure, and compliance. Leadership shapes culture, and culture shapes outcomes.

I've observed that many correctional leaders fall into one of two categories: they are either **nearsighted** or **farsighted** in their leadership approach.

Nearsighted leadership focuses on what's right in front of them: daily operations, immediate problems, short-term wins.

- **Strength:** Good at handling urgent matters and staying grounded.

- **Weakness:** May miss long-term strategy, broader vision, or future challenges.

Farsighted leadership focuses on big-picture goals, future planning, and vision.

- **Strength:** Helps steer the organization toward long-term success and innovation.
- **Weakness:** May lose touch with day-to-day realities, staff concerns, or operational details.

The strongest leaders **balance both**. They develop "20/20 vision" for their organization. You need to see what's right in front of you (your team's needs, current operations), and what's further down the road (growth, vision, sustainability). If you over-focus on one at the expense of the other, leadership gets out of alignment, just like vision problems.

I can remember working under both types of leaders. Some were so focused on enforcing policy that they ignored the people behind those policies. Others were obsessed with keeping the facility "quiet" with no incidents so that upper managers would assume everything was fine. But in both cases, the reality was far from healthy. Staff were burned out from long hours and pushed beyond their limits with too few resources. Detainees felt hopeless and disconnected. What looked "calm" on paper was actually an unhealthy facility in decline.

Modern Jail Leadership

Measuring Jail Health: More Than Audit Scores

So how do leaders really know if their facility is healthy? You can't rely on audit reports alone. Passing an ACA, NCCHC, or PREA audit is important, but it only captures a moment in time. True jail health is something leaders must measure every day through the lived experiences of staff and detainees.

I always tell leaders: *don't just read the reports, read the culture.* Look at how people interact. Listen to the tone of the facility. Pay attention to what your staff and detainees are saying and what they aren't saying.

Every leader brings their own personality to the role, and that naturally shapes leadership style. But one thing is consistent across the best leaders I've observed: **they get out of their office and manage by walking around.** You can't hear your facility's heartbeat from behind a desk. Walking the floors, talking with staff and detainees, seeing the operations firsthand—this is where you find the truth about your organization.

Here are key areas I believe every jail leader should monitor, especially while managing by walking:

- **Staff morale and retention.** Are people staying because they believe in the mission, or because they feel stuck? High turnover is always a red flag.
- **Trends in use-of-force, grievances, and sick leave.** Rising numbers here usually reflect deeper cultural problems.

- **Staff-inmate interactions.** Are officers engaging with professionalism and respect? Or do you see cynicism, tension, or apathy on the floor?
- **Inmate grievances and feedback.** Patterns of legitimate complaints about safety, health care, or treatment signal an unhealthy culture.
- **Facility "tone."** What does the facility feel like? I've always believed: *you can walk into a jail and "feel" the tone within the first five minutes.*
- **Community perception.** How is your jail seen by courts, health providers, advocates, and local media? If a facility is isolating itself, that's a risk.

Great leadership demands listening, observing, and acting on both data and human experience. When leaders pay close attention to these signs, they can address cultural issues before they turn into major crises. Because one thing is certain: problems that go unaddressed will surface eventually, and when they do, the cost is high.

Risks of an Unhealthy Jail Culture

An unhealthy jail culture rarely starts with a single event; it's the slow erosion of trust, morale, and accountability over time. When leadership fails to nurture the culture of the facility, the signs may not be obvious at first. But make no mistake: an unhealthy culture carries very real risks for staff, for detainees, and for the agency.

One of the first red flags is staffing instability. In a toxic environment, good staff won't stay. High turnover becomes the norm, and new hires often struggle to thrive. The remaining staff face burnout, long shifts, and increasing frustration—which only deepens the cycle.

Liability risk also increases sharply. Facilities with unhealthy cultures tend to see more use-of-force incidents, more grievances, more civil suits, and—in the worst cases—DOJ involvement or consent decrees. I've seen agencies where leadership ignored cultural warning signs, only to face massive legal and financial consequences later.

Public trust erodes as well. Jails operate within a larger community ecosystem. When the culture is poor, relationships with courts, public defenders, service providers, and the media become strained. Family members of staff begin to criticize the work environment and worry about their loved ones.

I remember taking over a facility that had almost every issue imaginable. During those early days, my own family members would ask, "Are you sure this is the right place for you to work? Do you really think you can turn this around? That jail has had problems for years." Those were fair questions because the public perception had been shaped by years of dysfunction. The facility was no longer seen as a professional, ethical part of the justice system. Instead, it was isolated and targeted by advocacy groups and local press.

And inside the walls, the human cost is high. Staff begin to disengage emotionally. Professionalism fades. Detainees feel unsafe, unheard, and neglected. Small problems escalate into major incidents. And leadership ends up spending all its time reacting to crises because the culture was never actively led in the first place.

The good news? Culture can be turned around. But it takes intentional leadership. Leaders must first acknowledge where things stand and then commit to modeling, teaching, and reinforcing the kind of culture they want to see. Because if leaders don't define the culture, the culture will define itself, and the risks will follow.

Building a Culture of Wellness, Safety, and Accountability

Turning around culture, or building it strong from the start, takes more than policies and memos. It takes leadership that is visible, intentional, and committed to the long game. Culture doesn't shift overnight, but it *can* shift. And when it does, the entire facility changes.

In my experience, the most effective way to start building a healthy culture is simple: **show up and listen**. Leadership presence matters. Walking the floors, talking with staff, having real conversations—

this is how you begin to understand the culture you have, and what needs to change.

From there, leaders must model the behaviors they expect to see: **respect, professionalism, and accountability**. These aren't values written on a poster. They are demonstrated every day by how leadership speaks and acts. When staff see leaders holding themselves to high standards, they will follow. When they see hypocrisy or excuses, they will disengage.

To build a culture of wellness, safety, and accountability, I encourage leaders to focus on these actions:

- **Be visible and present.** Walk the facility regularly (I know I've said this before, *HINT!*). Talk to staff at every level. Let people see leadership engaged and invested.
- **Communicate clearly and consistently.** People need to know what is expected, what is valued, and how success will be measured. Silence breeds confusion and mistrust.
- **Recognize staff contributions.** Public praise and private appreciation go a long way in building morale. People want to know their work matters.
- **Hold consistent accountability.** Fair, consistent discipline builds trust. Favoritism or inconsistent enforcement destroys it.

- **Invest in wellness initiatives.** Staff wellness impacts every part of the facility. Support programs that address stress, mental health, and work-life balance. **Allow staff to attend training they value. Build individuals, so they can help you build the culture.**
- **Build partnerships with external agencies.** No facility succeeds in isolation. Strong relationships with healthcare providers, mental health professionals, courts, and community partners create a more supportive and effective system.

Building a healthy culture is a leadership responsibility, one that requires daily attention. When leaders focus on wellness, safety, and accountability, the results ripple outward: staff become more engaged, detainees feel more secure, and the entire facility moves toward resilience and professionalism.

The Ongoing Leadership Challenge

Building and maintaining a healthy facility is not a one-time effort; it's an ongoing leadership challenge. Culture is not something that can be fixed and then forgotten. It is dynamic. It shifts with staff turnover, leadership changes, new pressures, and emerging needs. The moment a leader takes their eyes off culture, the organization will begin to drift, often in the wrong direction.

That's why I believe one of the most important traits for a correctional leader is consistency. You must show up, every day, with intention. You must continue to listen, to model the right behaviors, to reinforce expectations, and to invest in the people who make the facility run. You cannot "inspect" culture into a facility; **you have to lead it.**

The best leaders I've worked with and the kind of leader I strive to be never get comfortable. They understand that culture requires constant attention. They ask themselves regularly, "What kind of facility are we creating today? What is my staff seeing and hearing from me? What behaviors am I rewarding, and what behaviors am I tolerating?"

Leadership at this level requires flexibility. As John Maxwell teaches, "A leader is one who knows the way, goes the way, and shows the way." Sometimes, that means leading from the front and setting the vision. Sometimes, it means walking alongside staff, coaching and encouraging. And sometimes, it means stepping behind and letting others lead while you support and develop them.

Leadership is not about control; it's about influence. And in this field, done well, it can change lives. You create a facility where staff feel valued, where detainees are treated with dignity, and where the community can trust that the jail is a place of professionalism and accountability.

That is the ongoing leadership challenge—and opportunity—that today's correctional leaders must embrace.

Reflection Questions

1. How would you honestly assess the current culture of your facility?
2. What actions could you take this month to strengthen trust, wellness, and accountability in your team?
3. In what ways are you modeling the culture you want your staff to embrace?
4. Are there signs of disengagement or burnout you need to address right now?
5. Who are your external partners and how strong are those relationships today?

Chapter 3

BUILDING CULTURE THROUGH LEADERSHIP

"The leader is the one who sets the tone for the entire organization. Culture is not created by what you write—it's created by what you tolerate and what you celebrate."
Craig Groeschel

"You can't 'talk' culture into being—you have to live it, reinforce it, and lead it through every action."
Crayman J. Harvey

"Presence matters. You can't lead a correctional facility from behind a closed door."
Crayman J. Harvey

Leadership defines culture. You can have the best policies, the best training, and the cleanest audits—but if leadership is weak, absent, or inconsistent, the culture will reflect that. In every jail or detention facility I've worked in, whether as an officer, a manager, or a consultant, the culture always mirrored the tone set by leadership. If the leadership team is visible, trustworthy, and consistent, the facility runs smoother. Staff are more engaged, detainees respond better, and accountability is stronger. But when leadership is disconnected or disengaged, the cracks start to show, and culture starts to drift in the wrong direction. That's why I believe one of the most important responsibilities of any jail leader is to build culture every single day.

Let me pause right here because I should offer a disclaimer: changing culture is hard work. A leader with a lazy will cannot and will not change a culture for the better. Culture change demands energy, consistency, and resolve. You can't "talk" culture into being. You have to live it, reinforce it, and lead it through every action. If you're not ready to do that work, the culture won't move. If you are, the rewards can be transformational, not just for the facility, but for the people inside it.

Leadership Sets the Tone

In corrections, the leadership tone is everything. Over time, your staff and detainees will reflect what they see in you, whether that reflection is positive or negative. You can't "hide" your leadership style in this environment. Every action (and inaction) sends a message about what is valued, what is tolerated, and what is ignored.

When a leader sets a tone of professionalism, accountability, and respect, staff will naturally raise their own standards. Detainees will notice the difference as well. I've seen facilities where culture shifted dramatically, not because of a new policy manual, but because leadership modeled the behaviors they wanted to see.

On the other hand, when leadership tolerates low standards, excuses poor behavior, or disappears when problems arise, staff will follow suit. They'll start to think, *If leadership doesn't care, why should I?* And culture will drift, usually in the wrong direction.

It's simple, but powerful: **your facility becomes a reflection of your leadership**. Good leadership builds a culture where people want to do their best work and where professional pride grows. Poor leadership creates an environment where people check out, cut corners, or give in to cynicism.

I remember a time when I took over a facility as director that was designed for a **direct supervision model**, where staff members were inside housing units

24/7 to manage detainees directly. This model is popular across the country because it lowers incidents and improves staff-inmate rapport.

But over time, this particular facility had drifted away from that model without adopting a clear alternative. The result? **Contraband increased. Property destruction escalated. And perhaps most damaging of all, staff-to-inmate rapport had dissolved.**

Recognizing how serious this cultural drift was, I implemented what I called **Command Walkthroughs.** Every Wednesday, my command staff, along with key partners like mental health, medical, and kitchen managers, conducted full-facility walkthroughs. We intentionally connected with both staff and detainees, building trust and visibility.

For anyone thinking, *My facility is too big. We couldn't do that,"* let me say this was an 1,100-bed facility with 18 housing units, and it was overcrowded. **It can be done—if leadership wants it done.**

And the change was immediate. Detainees began to trust the leadership team again. Staff felt visible and supported by executive management. Morale started to shift. The tone of the facility changed, not because of a memo, but because leadership was present and engaged.

Modern Jail Leadership

Visibility and Approachability

In corrections, leadership visibility is not optional—it's essential. You can't lead from behind a closed office door. If staff never see you, if detainees only hear your name but never see your face, your leadership presence is already diminished. And with it, your influence on culture will suffer.

Presence matters. People follow what they see, not just what they hear. When leadership is visible—walking the facility, interacting with staff, engaging detainees when appropriate—trust grows. Communication opens up. You start to hear things you wouldn't hear in formal meetings, and you start to see the tone of your facility with your own eyes, not just through reports.

Approachability matters just as much. Staff should feel comfortable coming to leadership with concerns, ideas, or feedback. When leadership is unapproachable because of ego, distance, or fear, communication shuts down. The small problems you could have solved early grow into bigger issues that damage morale and operations.

In my experience, visibility + approachability = trust. And trust is the foundation of a healthy culture. When people trust leadership, they engage. When they don't, they disconnect.

One thing I always remind myself as a director: **I am part of the team not the owner.** The owner is the county, state, or government entity. As a team member, I need to look like my team, be embedded with my team, and help shape a positive culture alongside them.

Small but intentional actions make a big impact. I make it a point to eat lunch in the cafeteria with staff. I drink coffee in the breakroom with staff. I've even worn the same uniform they do to show that I stand with them, not above them. These simple actions build trust, break down walls, and reinforce the idea that leadership is part of the team not separate from it.

Communication That Builds Culture

In corrections, communication is one of the most powerful tools a leader has for shaping culture. And yet, poor communication is one of the most common leadership failures I see across facilities. You cannot expect staff to align with your vision if they don't understand it. You cannot expect professionalism if expectations are unclear. And you cannot build trust if your words don't match your actions.

Good communication in a correctional environment is more than passing along memos or policy updates. It is about **setting tone, reinforcing values, and creating clarity** every day, in both formal and informal ways.

Leaders should consistently communicate what matters most: What we stand for here, What we value as a team, What is expected from every staff member,

Modern Jail Leadership

How success is defined and celebrated, How accountability is applied—fairly and consistently

I've seen facilities where leadership was technically "present," but communication was vague, inconsistent, or reactive. Staff were left guessing. Rumors spread. Morale eroded. On the other hand, when leaders communicate openly, consistently, and with purpose, culture strengthens. People know where the ship is headed, and they know they are part of that mission.

In my own leadership, I try to communicate in layers:

- **Facility-wide messaging**: regular briefings, emails, shift meetings
- **Informal hallway conversations**: "small talk" that builds relationships
- **One-on-one encouragement and coaching**, (you'll hear more about this later)
- **Consistent visibility on the floor**, letting actions reinforce words

When staff hear one thing in a meeting and see the same message modeled in leadership behavior, culture begins to change. But when leadership says one thing and does another, trust fractures, and culture suffers.

The bottom line is simple: **You cannot build culture without communication**, and what is communicated must be intentional not just reactive when something goes wrong.

Coaching and Developing Your People

In corrections, it's easy for leadership to slip into a "directive" style: just giving orders, correcting mistakes, moving from one crisis to the next. But real leadership is not just about directing; it's about developing. Strong leaders don't just tell staff what to do. Instead, they build people, and when you build people, you build culture.

One of the most powerful ways to shape culture is through coaching, consistent, everyday coaching that helps staff grow, learn, and lead. Too often, leadership thinks coaching is something that only happens in formal evaluations or training sessions. But the best coaching happens in the daily moments: a conversation after shift, feedback in the field, an encouraging word when someone is struggling, or a quiet correction when standards aren't being met.

In my experience, great leaders do this naturally. They **see staff as people first**, people with potential, not just bodies to fill posts. And when staff know that leadership is invested in their growth, trust goes up, morale goes up, and performance follows.

I've also learned this: if you want to build culture, you have to build leaders within your facility. You can't do it alone. You need frontline staff, corporals, sergeants, and lieutenants who understand the culture you are working to create and who will help reinforce it every day.

That's why I make it a priority to coach and develop my people, especially those with leadership potential. I want them to know that their growth matters. I want them to see themselves as part of the future of the facility because when leadership development is built into your culture, professionalism and pride grow, and the culture strengthens from the inside out.

Modeling Accountability

One of the clearest ways leadership shapes culture is through accountability and not just how you hold others accountable, but how you hold yourself accountable first. In corrections, staff pay close attention to what leadership tolerates and what leadership demonstrates. If there's one thing I've seen over and over: **the culture of the facility will follow the example of leadership.**

You can say that professionalism, respect, and integrity matter, but if you look the other way when standards slip, you send a very different message. You can tell staff that accountability is important, but if leadership excuses poor behavior from certain people, or applies discipline inconsistently, trust will collapse. What the leader tolerates, the culture will embrace.

That's why **modeling accountability starts with you**. Leaders must hold themselves to the highest standards, first in attitude, then in actions. Staff will notice. They will model what they see.

Fair and consistent accountability is key:

- **Fair**: No favoritism. No "special rules" for certain staff. The same standard applies to everyone.
- **Consistent**: Not just during an audit cycle, not just after an incident, but every day.

I always remind my leadership teams: **you don't build trust through punishment. You build it through fairness and consistency.** Staff are willing to be held accountable when they know it will be done fairly and when they see that leadership holds itself accountable as well.

But if accountability is uneven, if it only applies when convenient, professionalism will erode, morale will drop, and your culture will suffer. Strong leaders model the accountability they expect. And when they do, the facility becomes a place where standards are respected, not just written in a binder.

Handling Cultural Drift

Culture is not "set and forget." It shifts constantly, sometimes in small ways that are easy to miss. I call this **cultural drift**, and if leaders aren't watching for it, even a strong culture can slowly slide into one that no longer reflects your values.

Drift usually starts with small things:

- Staff cutting corners because they're burned out
- Minor policy violations being overlooked "just this once"
- Cynicism or negativity creeping into shift conversations
- New hires picking up bad habits because no one corrected them

Left unchecked, these small things grow. And before you know it, the culture you worked hard to build is no longer there. That's why leaders must stay tuned in—watching for the signs of drift and acting early.

So how do you do it?

- **Stay connected.** Regularly walk the facility. Talk to staff. Listen carefully. The first signs of drift won't show up in a report; they'll show up in what you hear and see on the floor.
- **Ask the right questions.** How is staff feeling about the work? Are standards being followed consistently? What messages are being sent intentionally or unintentionally?
- **Address issues early.** It's easier to correct drift when it's small. The longer you wait, the harder it is to pull culture back on course.

- **Use feedback loops.** Encourage honest feedback from all levels: line staff, supervisors, support staff. Let people know you want to hear when things are starting to slide and then act on what you hear.

Culture drift happens in every facility—it's natural. But strong leaders recognize it, address it, and realign their team before the drift becomes the new norm. The goal is to **lead culture actively, not passively, every single day.**

The Leader's Legacy

Every leader leaves a legacy, whether they realize it or not. Long after you move on from a facility, the culture you built (or failed to build) will remain. Staff will remember how it felt to work under your leadership. The facility's tone, expectations, and professionalism will either reflect the culture you helped shape or reflect the drift you allowed.

That's why it's so important for correctional leaders to think beyond the day-to-day. Ask yourself:

- What do I want this facility to feel like six months after I leave? One year? Five years?
- What kind of leadership culture am I building for those who will follow me?

If the culture is built only on your presence, it will fade when you're gone. But if you build leadership into your team—if you coach, develop, and empower others to carry the culture forward—your influence will last.

The best leaders don't just run a facility well during their time in the chair. They leave it better for the next leader, and the next generation of staff. That's the kind of legacy I try to leave. And that's the kind of leadership that will truly change corrections for the better.

Because in the end, policies may change, audits may come and go, but culture lasts. And leadership defines culture.

Reflection Questions

1. How would your staff describe your leadership tone today?
2. What small daily actions are you taking to build trust and culture?
3. Are you modeling the accountability and professionalism you want your staff to follow?
4. How do you listen for—and address—early signs of cultural drift?
5. What leadership legacy do you want to leave in your facility?

Chapter 4

LEADING THROUGH CRISIS AND CHANGE

"Anyone can hold the helm when the sea is calm."
Publilius Syrus

"Leadership is not about chasing perfection—it's about steady, consistent progress over time."
Crayman J. Harvey

The Reality of Crisis in Corrections

If you lead in corrections long enough, you will face crisis. It's not a question of *if* but *when*. Whether it's a staffing emergency, a critical incident, a public health outbreak, a civil lawsuit, or federal investigation, corrections leadership is tested most in moments of adversity. And how you lead during those times will

Modern Jail Leadership

shape your culture far more than anything you say during calm periods.

I've been through this personally. When I served as director of the Alvin S. Glenn Detention Center in Richland County, South Carolina, we faced one of the most difficult periods any facility can experience. The U.S. Department of Justice issued a findings report on the facility, citing constitutional violations, systemic staffing problems, unsafe conditions, and deteriorating infrastructure. The facility was under national scrutiny, the media coverage was relentless, and the pressure on leadership, staff, and detainees was intense.

Yet even in the middle of that storm, I knew leadership presence mattered more than ever. You can't disappear in crisis; you have to lean in. We initiated major reforms: a $100 million renovation project to address infrastructure needs, the creation of a dedicated mental health unit to better serve detainees, and steps to improve staff morale and visibility. I made it a point to be present on the floor, communicate openly, and support my team through the chaos.

Was it easy? No. In fact, it was one of the hardest leadership challenges of my career. After helping move some key reforms forward, I chose to transition out, knowing the work would be ongoing. I later accepted the role of director at Kershaw County Detention Center, carrying forward hard-earned lessons about leadership in times of crisis.

I share this not to highlight difficulties but to say this: crisis will test your leadership, and it will shape you. How you show up for your team during those moments matters, and your facility's culture will remember it long after the crisis passes.

Maintaining Leadership Presence During Crisis

In corrections, how a leader shows up during crisis is often remembered far longer than what they do during routine operations. Crisis moments reveal leadership character, not just to staff, but to the entire facility.

When crisis hits—whether it's a critical incident, media scrutiny, staffing emergency, or federal oversight—**leaders must stay visible.** The worst thing a leader can do is disappear into an office or limit communication to just a few managers. In times of stress, your team needs to see leadership on the floor, in the housing units, walking the post, and standing with them.

Presence matters even more in these moments because staff are watching for cues: *Is leadership calm? Is leadership communicating? Does leadership have a plan, and are they standing with us?*

When leadership stays visible and present, it sends a clear message: *we are in this together.* Staff feel supported. They stay engaged. They follow the tone leadership sets.

Modern Jail Leadership

During the DOJ period at Alvin S. Glenn, I made it a priority to be present on the floor every day. Even when it would have been easier to hide behind emails or legal meetings, I knew that visible leadership was non-negotiable. Staff needed to see me showing up as part of the team, not as a figurehead. The message was simple: *I'm here. We'll get through this together.*

In any crisis, leadership visibility does two things:

- **It calms the staff.** When people feel informed and supported, fear and rumor are reduced.
- **It stabilizes the culture.** In a crisis, culture can either fracture or strengthen, depending on how leadership responds.

You cannot lead a facility through crisis from behind a desk. You lead through presence, through calm words, clear communication, and steady action.

Communicating Transparently in Difficult Times

In crisis, **how you communicate will define how your team responds.** The natural tendency for many leaders is to either pull back communication, worried about saying the wrong thing, or to rely too much on official statements that don't feel human to the people doing the work.

But in corrections, where staff operate in high-stress environments even on a normal day, the absence of clear communication during crisis only fuels fear, rumor, and division. **Silence in crisis is dangerous.** Staff will fill in the blanks with their own interpretations, and usually, those interpretations lean negative.

That's why transparent, regular communication is key. In difficult times, **you can't communicate too much,** and you must be clear about what is known, what is not yet known, and what steps leadership is taking. People don't expect leaders to have all the answers, but they do expect honesty.

During the DOJ period at Alvin S. Glenn, I made it a priority to communicate consistently:

- Updates on what was happening, even when news was difficult
- Reassurance about the mission and the team's role
- Acknowledgment of stress and appreciation for staff holding the line
- A calm, steady tone because fear spreads fast but so does calm

One of the things I learned is this: **when people feel informed, they stay engaged**, even in adversity. When they feel in the dark, disengagement follows fast.

In crisis, your words carry more weight than ever, and they are needed more than ever. Communicate early, communicate often, and communicate with honesty and care. Because trust is built or lost in these moments.

Modern Jail Leadership

Resilience for Leadership Teams

Crisis tests not only the culture of a facility; it tests the leadership team itself. When long hours, public scrutiny, and constant challenges pile up, even the strongest leaders can feel the strain. That's why resilience, both personal and team-wide, is critical during extended periods of crisis or change.

As a leader, it's easy to focus all your energy on supporting the staff and forget to support the leadership team. But if your lieutenants, captains, command staff, and frontline supervisors start to burn out, the cracks will spread quickly through the entire organization. **Leaders must take care of each other.**

Here are a few things I've learned about building leadership resilience during crisis:

- **Acknowledge the strain.** Leadership is not about pretending everything is fine. Let your team know it's okay to feel the weight and that you see their effort.
- **Encourage open conversation.** Regular check-ins with leadership team members help surface stress points before they become breaking points. Sometimes just having space to talk helps release the pressure.
- **Model work-life balance.** If you're working 14-hour days, 7 days a week, your team will feel pressured to do the same, and burnout will follow. It's okay to show balance, and to give

your leaders permission to rest and recharge when needed.
- **Invest in peer support.** Encourage leaders to support one another. A strong command team will carry each other through tough seasons and come out stronger.
- **Debrief, learn, and adapt.** After intense incidents, build time for leadership debriefs. What worked? What didn't? What can we learn? Crisis can grow leadership if you let it.

Leadership resilience starts at the top, but it ripples outward. When the leadership team remains steady, staff feel it. When leadership fractures under stress, the entire facility suffers.

Strong leadership teams aren't perfect, but they support each other, learn through crisis, and come out stronger on the other side.

Using Crisis as a Leadership Opportunity

Every crisis has two sides: the challenge and the opportunity. The challenge is obvious: the stress, the risk, the scrutiny, the uncertainty. But many leaders miss the opportunity because **crisis moments can either fracture a team or strengthen it.**

Modern Jail Leadership

When leadership responds well, crisis becomes a chance to:
- Build trust
- Reinforce values
- Develop new leaders
- Strengthen relationships with partners and the community
- Create a more resilient and professional culture

How? By how you lead in the moment:
- **Stay present.** Crisis is not the time to disappear.
- **Communicate honestly.** People will remember how you spoke to them during hard times.
- **Model calm and confidence.** Fear spreads fast, but so does steady leadership.
- **Recognize effort.** Staff working through crisis need to hear that their efforts are seen and appreciated.

One thing I've learned: **culture shows up in crisis, but leadership shapes how it survives.** When you lead well through adversity, you build a kind of loyalty, trust, and pride that lasts far beyond the crisis itself. Staff remember who stood with them. Morale can actually grow, not despite the crisis, but because of how leadership carried the team through it.

Some of the strongest leadership teams I've worked with were forged during hard times, when leaders leaned in, supported one another, and led with integrity. Crisis moments pass, but the leadership impact will be felt long after.

Leading Change in a Resistant Culture

In corrections, change is hard. It's not because people in this profession are stubborn. It's because the work is demanding, the environment is high-risk, and there is comfort in routine. People want to know what to expect, and when change comes, the first instinct is often resistance.

"We've always done it this way."

"That won't work here."

"Why fix what isn't broken?"

If you've led in this field long enough, you've heard all of those. And that's normal. But as leaders, we know this: **if you're not moving forward, you're falling behind.** Facilities that resist change too long end up reacting to crisis instead of building resilience.

When I led the Alvin S. Glenn Detention Center through some of the hardest years in its history, one of the most difficult—and most important—decisions I made was to shut down the facility's Special Housing Unit (SHU), historically used for solitary confinement.

There was plenty of resistance to that decision. Some staff members were concerned about losing a traditional tool. Some worried about managing the most difficult detainees without the old SHU model. But I knew **culture would not change if we didn't change the environment and practices driving that culture.**

We replaced the SHU with **specialized units**, mental health care, medical treatment, older detainees, and behavior management units, built around targeted care instead of isolation. That change not only aligned the facility with modern standards; it sent a message to staff and detainees alike about what we valued: safety, dignity, and professionalism.

Was it easy? No. Leading that change required clear communication, listening to concerns, and staying consistent because resistance was real. But over time, the culture began to shift. Staff started to embrace the new model. And most importantly, outcomes began to improve.

That's what I've learned about leading change in a resistant culture:

- **Bring people into the process.** People will support what they help create.
- **Explain the why.** People will resist change they don't understand.
- **Start with small wins.** Build momentum through success.

- **Be consistent.** Stay the course because change takes time.
- **Celebrate progress.** Highlight the wins that prove the value of change.

Change is never easy, but it's essential. And the leader's job is not to avoid resistance; it's to **lead through it.**

The Long View: Leadership Through Cycles of Change

One of the most important lessons I've learned in this work is **change is not a one-time event; it's a cycle.** In corrections, you are always leading through cycles of change. Leadership teams change. Political environments change. Staffing levels shift. Policies evolve. Community expectations grow. And with every new challenge comes a new opportunity or a new risk, depending on how leadership responds.

The best leaders I've seen, the ones I respect the most, keep the long view in mind. They know that leadership is about more than today's incident, today's headline, or today's audit. It's about building a facility that is resilient, professional, and prepared for the next season, even after they're gone.

In your career, you will lead through seasons of crisis. You will lead through resistance. You will lead through rebuilding. The key is to understand that leadership is not about chasing perfection. It's about steady, consistent progress over time. It's about leaving the facility better than you found it and helping your people grow along the way.

I often remind my teams that *leadership is not about you. It's about the people you serve: the staff, the detainees, and the community—and the culture you will leave behind when your chapter here is done.*

In every facility I've led, from times of calm to times of crisis, that long view has helped guide my leadership. Because in this field, the work is never really finished. The next leader will pick up where you leave off. And your legacy will live in the culture you helped shape for better or worse.

Lead with the long view. Your team and your facility will be stronger for it.

Reflection Questions

1. How does your leadership presence impact your team during times of crisis or change?
2. What steps are you taking to build resilience in yourself and in your leadership team?
3. How are you communicating during difficult seasons? Are you building trust or leaving gaps?
4. Where do you see cultural resistance in your facility, and how can you lead through it?

5. What long-term leadership legacy are you working toward, and what will you leave behind when you move on?

Chapter 5

BALANCING SECURITY, HEALTH, AND REHABILITATION

"Security is the foundation, but dignity, care, and rehabilitation help build the house."
Crayman J. Harvey

The Triple Mission of Today's Jail

For too long, jails in the United States have operated with a "custody first, everything else second" mindset. Security dominated operations, and to an extent, it must. In a correctional environment, safety and control provide the foundation for everything else. Without it, nothing else works.

But as I wrote in an article for the American Jail Association, "Security has long predominated in U.S. correctional operations—but today's leaders must adopt a holistic model that balances custody with care and rehabilitation."

That's the reality of today's jails: **we are asked to serve a triple mission,** and it takes strong leadership to balance it:

- **Security.** Keeping the facility safe and controlled
- **Health care.** Addressing physical and mental health needs
- **Rehabilitation and re-entry.** Preparing detainees to return to the community better than they arrived

These missions sometimes feel in tension. Security staff may fear that focusing too much on programming or health will weaken control. Health partners may feel the custody side resists needed change. But leadership must guide the team to understand that **these priorities are not in competition; they are interdependent.**

Facilities that over-focus on security alone become brittle: staff burn out, legal risk grows, and the public loses trust. Facilities that neglect security in the name of programming lose safety and control, and no one thrives. The best-led jails build balance where **safety enables care, care builds trust, and trust enables rehabilitation.**

Modern Jail Leadership

Why Balance Matters

When security dominates a jail's mission to the exclusion of everything else, negative outcomes follow. Staff burnout increases. Tension between officers and detainees rises. Legal risk grows. And public trust erodes.

On the other hand, when facilities neglect security in pursuit of programming or outside praise, chaos can take hold, undermining both safety and services. **Balance is not just a goal. It's a necessity.**

As I wrote in my article for the American Jail Association, "Leaders in progressive jails must work to balance custody, care, and rehabilitation—recognizing that these priorities strengthen one another when led well."

Facilities that maintain that balance see real benefits:

- Lower use-of-force incidents
- Better staff morale and retention
- Stronger partnerships with courts, providers, and the community
- Improved re-entry outcomes, which reduces recidivism
- Fewer legal challenges and regulatory risks

Why? Because when staff understand that their role is bigger than just "holding the line," that they are part of a team providing care and preparing detainees for success, their professionalism increases. And when detainees see leadership committed to dignity and accountability, trust grows, and behavior improves.

I've seen this firsthand: in facilities that lean too far toward custody alone, morale crumbles. In balanced facilities, staff take pride in the work because they see how it matters beyond today's shift.

That's why leadership must set the tone: *Security is the foundation but not the house.* The house must also include health and rehabilitation because that is what builds a facility that truly serves the community.

Leadership Role in Driving Balance

Balancing custody, care, and rehabilitation doesn't happen by accident. It happens because leadership makes it happen. In every facility I've worked in or consulted with, this truth holds: **the priorities of a jail reflect the priorities of its leadership.**

If leadership only talks about security, only measures custody outcomes, only rewards "old school" control, then that is what the culture will value and nothing more. Health care will be seen as someone else's job. Rehabilitation will be viewed as "extra," something nice, but not essential.

But when leadership sets the tone, when leaders communicate that *care and rehabilitation matter as much as custody*, the culture begins to shift. Officers start to see their role in health and re-entry. Health staff feel valued, not sidelined. And the community sees a facility that serves public safety in the broadest sense—not just warehousing people.

I always tell my teams, **If you don't lead balance, the facility will default to what's easiest—custody-only.** That's human nature. The stress of the job, the risk of the environment, the old habits of the field—they all pull the culture back toward "control first." It takes strong, intentional leadership to build a facility where staff are proud of *all* three missions.

And the message must be clear:

- Security keeps people safe.
- Health care meets basic human rights and public health needs.
- Rehabilitation prepares people to succeed after release, which ultimately protects the community.

Balanced leadership leads to balanced outcomes, and it is the leader's responsibility to drive that balance every day.

Building Partnerships for Health and Programming

No jail can successfully balance custody, care, and rehabilitation in isolation. **It takes partnerships.** Medical and mental health services, courts, probation, re-entry programs, housing providers—all of these systems must work together if we want jails to be places that build healthier people and safer communities.

As I wrote in my article for the American Jail Association, "Health care inside correctional facilities is a constitutional right—and a critical public health issue. Jails are not just temporary holding facilities; they are key touchpoints for addressing unmet health needs—including mental health, substance use, and chronic conditions."

When I led the closure of the Special Housing Unit (SHU) at Alvin S. Glenn and replaced it with specialized units for mental health care, medical treatment, older detainees, and behavior management, I saw firsthand how partnerships change outcomes. That transition required collaboration with medical providers, mental health professionals, classification officers, frontline custody staff, and community care networks for continuity after release.

Without those partnerships, the closure of SHU would not have improved outcomes. It would have created new risks. But by working together, the new units helped stabilize detainees who might otherwise have cycled through isolation or incidents.

Progressive leaders understand that **health care is not a distraction from the jail's mission. It is central to that mission.**

- It protects staff by reducing incidents and medical crises.
- It fulfills legal and ethical obligations.

- It prepares detainees for release, reducing post-release mortality and recidivism.
- And it strengthens public trust because a community can respect a facility that treats people with dignity and care.

Building these partnerships takes time. It takes trust between custody and care teams. It takes leadership commitment. But it is worth the effort—because **jails cannot do this work alone**.

Leading Staff Toward Balance

One of the hardest parts of building balance in a facility is helping **staff see their role** in all three missions, not just custody. Many officers enter the field believing their only job is to "keep control." And for years, that was often the message reinforced: *security first, everything else second, if at all.*

But in today's jails, that mindset is not enough. Officers must be able to operate professionally in an environment that balances **safety, health care, and rehabilitation**. And it's leadership's job to coach staff toward that vision.

This doesn't happen through one training or one memo. It happens through leadership presence, daily conversations, recognition of the right behaviors, and reinforcement over time. I've learned that if you want staff to buy into a balanced mission, you have to:

- **Talk about it.** Make clear that care and rehabilitation are not "extra." They are part of our job.
- **Model it.** Interact with medical, mental health, and re-entry staff with professionalism and respect—because your tone sets the tone.
- **Coach staff in real time.** When you see an officer handle a difficult medical situation well, call it out and praise it. When someone shows empathy or initiative, recognize it.
- **Address resistance.** Don't let negativity or dismissive attitudes toward care and programming go unchecked. Address it early, coach it forward.
- **Build interdisciplinary teams.** Encourage custody staff to partner with care providers, classification, and programming staff—because collaboration strengthens culture.

When leadership commits to this, the culture shifts. Officers begin to see their role in the bigger mission. They develop professional pride not just in keeping order—but in being part of a team that helps people leave the facility healthier than they came in.

And that's the kind of leadership we need: officers who understand that **security is the foundation—but dignity, care, and rehabilitation help build the house.**

Modern Jail Leadership

The Outcomes of Balanced Leadership

When a facility is led with balance, where custody, care, and rehabilitation all matter, the results show up everywhere. You can feel it in the tone of the facility. You can see it in the professionalism of the staff. You can hear it in how the community talks about the jail.

Here's what I've seen in facilities that embrace balanced leadership:

- **Better morale.** When staff know their work matters beyond just keeping order, they take greater pride in it. They see themselves as part of something bigger, serving not only the jail but the community.
- **Lower risk.** Healthier detainees mean fewer crises. A balanced culture reduces use-of-force incidents, medical emergencies, and legal exposure.
- **Improved public trust.** Communities respect a facility that treats people with dignity and provides real opportunities for rehabilitation. Public perception matters, and balanced leadership earns that respect.
- **Stronger partnerships.** Courts, health providers, and re-entry programs are more willing to collaborate with a facility that demonstrates professional balance. You can't build good partnerships from a custody-only culture.

- **Better outcomes for detainees.** Ultimately, balanced leadership helps people leave the facility healthier, more stable, and more connected to services, which reduces recidivism and protects public safety long after release.

I often remind my teams that **what we do inside these walls matters outside these walls.** Balanced leadership makes that impact positive for staff, for detainees, for the justice system, and for the community.

Reflection Questions

1. How balanced is your facility today between security, health care, and rehabilitation?
2. How are you setting the tone for balanced leadership through your own actions?
3. Where are the gaps, and what partnerships could help strengthen balance?
4. How are you helping staff understand their role beyond just custody?
5. What one step could you take this month to move your facility closer to true balance?

Chapter 6

HIRING, TRAINING, AND DEVELOPING PEOPLE

"You don't build a business; you build people. And then people build the business."
Zig Ziglar

"You don't just manage a jail—you lead people. And those people are the heart of everything your facility will become."
Crayman J. Harvey

Why People Are the Heart of the Facility

In every facility I've led or consulted with, one truth holds: culture lives in people, not paper. Policies, procedures, or mission statements on the wall don't run the jail. The staff you hire, train, and develop do.

Hire poorly and fail to invest in development, and you will see a culture of burnout, turnover, and misconduct. Hire with intention, train with purpose, and develop leaders at every level, and you will see morale, professionalism, and outcomes rise. **Culture lives in the people**, and culture drives outcomes, good or bad.

I've seen facilities where the hiring pipeline was "fill the vacancies fast," and the result was a cycle of staff turnover, low morale, and misconduct. I've also seen facilities where leadership invested in hiring for values, trained with purpose, and built leadership at every level, and the difference in morale, professionalism, and outcomes was immediate.

If you want a healthy, resilient, and professional facility, **you must start with your people**.

- Hire for integrity and values.
- Train with purpose.
- Develop leaders at every level.
- Care for the wellness of your team.

Because the team you build today is the future of your facility. And leadership must lead that work—you can't delegate culture.

Hiring for More Than a Badge

In corrections, **who you hire matters more than almost anything else you do as a leader.** You can have the best policies and updated procedures, but if you hire the wrong people—or if you hire the right people and fail to develop them—your facility's culture will suffer.

It's easy in today's staffing crisis to fall into the trap of hiring for numbers—"warm bodies to fill posts." But bodies don't build culture—people do. And the people you hire today become the culture of your facility tomorrow.

I learned this the hard way. In 2024, while leading a large facility, we faced an unprecedented series of staff arrests—more than **11 arrests in one year** for contraband and misconduct, including correctional officers and even a nurse. Charges ranged from smuggling drugs and phones to inappropriate inmate contact. The incidents drew national media and DOJ attention, and forced hard conversations about hiring, training, and accountability.

Those arrests weren't just about "bad apples." They reflected **systemic gaps**:

- Hiring that prioritized filling vacancies fast, without enough focus on values and professionalism
- Training gaps, especially in preparing staff for manipulation and stress

- A reactive, not proactive, culture around staff conduct and peer accountability

When leaders tolerate a culture of "get them in the door," problems grow fast. If you don't hire well, you can't build culture. And if you don't invest in developing your people—even good hires can drift in the wrong direction under pressure. Staffing pressure tempts leaders to "fill the post." Don't. Bodies don't build culture—people do. When you hire for speed over standards, you buy tomorrow's turnover and misconduct. You can train skills; you can't train integrity. Select for mindset, professionalism, and pride, then invest early and relentlessly in development.

That's why I tell leadership teams that **they can't train integrity; they have to hire it**. Look for mindset and values—not just test scores or academy hours. Prioritize professionalism and pride—not just filling a roster.

Ultimately, **the team you build is the future of your facility**.

Building a Professional Workforce

In corrections, professionalism must be built not assumed. **Too often, jails fall into a "warm bodies in posts" mindset**, filling vacancies with whoever passes the basic checks then hoping they survive on the floor. Hope, however, is not a leadership strategy. Culture will reflect whatever you tolerate in your hiring and onboarding process. New hires copy what leaders tolerate. From day one, communicate clearly who you are, what you expect, and what professionalism looks like in action. Correct drift early, reward what you want repeated, and make sure leadership visibility reinforces the standard.

I've seen facilities where staff were treated like numbers, and they acted like it. Turnover skyrocketed, morale crumbled, and misconduct followed. I've also seen facilities where leadership made it clear: **this is a professional environment, and we expect professionalism from day one.** The difference in tone and performance was night and day.

Building a professional workforce starts with leadership expectations. From hiring through onboarding, communicate clearly, "Here's who we are, and here's how we do business." Don't assume new hires understand the mission—teach it and reinforce it. Show that professionalism is valued and rewarded. Correct gaps early because staff will mirror what they see tolerated.

Leadership visibility matters most here. New hires watch leadership more than anyone else. If they see leaders modeling professionalism, in interactions with staff, detainees, partners, they will adopt that tone. If they see leadership tolerating poor behavior or disengagement, they will follow that example, too.

That's why I make it a priority during onboarding to:

- **Meet with every new hire** before they hit the floor
- **Walk the floor with new staff** and show presence
- **Reinforce values at every level** so staff know this is a place where standards matter

Because **you can't build culture without building people.** And your new hires today will either strengthen your facility or weaken it, depending on how you lead their development.

Modernizing Training and Onboarding

One of the biggest leadership gaps I see in corrections today is outdated training, especially for new staff. Too many agencies still rely on the old "war stories" and "trial by fire" approaches, where recruits learn most of their habits from whoever happens to be on shift.

Today's job is more complex than ever, however. There are mental health crises, trauma-informed care, substance use, de-escalation, legal risk, and public accountability.

If we want professionalism on the floor, we have to train for professionalism starting on day one. That means moving beyond basic policies and procedures and teaching the skills that actually shape culture:

- **Emotional intelligence**, helping staff manage their own stress and read situations
- **Communication**, learning how officers talk to detainees (and each other) affects outcomes every shift
- **Conflict de-escalation**, knowing how to prevent small tensions from becoming major incidents
- **Mental health awareness**, understanding the realities staff will face on the floor
- **Cultural humility**, treating all people with dignity, regardless of background

It also means investing in **your trainers and field training officers (FTOs)** because those who train the new hires *become the culture*. If senior staff are cynical, disengaged, or resistant to change, that's what new officers will pick up.

When I work with agencies today, I tell them that their onboarding is not just about "checking the boxes." It's truly about shaping their future culture. The investment you make up front in training and development will either strengthen your team for years or set you up for turnover, risk, and cultural drift.

Leadership must own this because if you delegate onboarding too far down, the tone gets lost, and in corrections, tone is everything.

Developing Leaders at Every Level

One of the biggest lessons I've learned is **you can't change culture alone; you need leaders at every level**. That's true whether you're running a small county jail or a large regional facility. If the only person driving professionalism is the director, the culture will crumble the minute that leader steps out of the room or out of the role.

Real culture change happens when you develop leaders—corporals, sergeants, lieutenants, FTOs—who carry the message forward every day. These are the people new hires watch. These are the people the rank-and-file will follow, for better or worse. That's why investing in leadership development at every level is critical:

- **Coach supervisors** not just in tasks but in leadership presence and tone
- **Train corporals and sergeants** so they understand their role isn't just enforcing rules—it's shaping culture
- **Mentor potential leaders**, spot talent early, and help it grow
- **Hold the line on expectations**, making sure the frontline leadership team models professionalism consistently

When I onboard new supervisors, I make it clear: **You are a leader now. People are watching you. You are shaping this culture with every action you take or don't take.**

One colleague I greatly respect, **Diana Knapp, MS, CCE, CJM**, takes this a step further. As Director of Corrections for Jackson County Detention Center (Kansas City, Missouri), 1st Vice President of the American Jail Association, and Chair of AJA's Corrections Leadership Committee, she teaches the importance of **setting a positive example, both on and off duty**.

Staff do not stop being a representative of the facility when they clock out. Their behavior in the community, on social media, and in everyday life shapes public trust and the professional identity of the agency.

In today's environment, **professionalism must extend beyond the badge**. Staff need to see leadership modeling that expectation and coaching it in others because in corrections, we can't afford the mindset of "that's just how they act off duty."

If we want to grow a professional culture that the public can respect and that staff are proud to represent, leadership at every level must set that tone **on and off duty**, every day. Ultimately, **you can't build culture alone, and you can't build it halfway**. You need leaders at every level to carry the message, model the standard, and reinforce the mission, whether in uniform or in the community.

Investing in Staff Wellness

If you want to build a professional, resilient workforce, you cannot ignore wellness. Staff wellness and retention go hand in hand. When leadership neglects wellness, morale erodes, burnout increases, and turnover rises—and culture suffers.

Correctional work is high-stress by nature with constant exposure to conflict, unpredictable shifts, understaffing, vicarious trauma from dealing with detainees in crisis, and pressure from public and legal scrutiny. No one is immune, not officers, not supervisors, not command staff. That's why leadership must treat wellness as **a core part of the mission** not an afterthought. In my own leadership experience, I've seen firsthand how investing in wellness improves performance:

- Staff stay more engaged and committed
- Incidents and sick time decrease
- Peer support improves
- Professional pride grows
- Retention stabilizes

Here are ways leaders can invest in wellness without waiting for a massive budget increase:

- **Talk about it.** Make wellness a leadership conversation, not just a side note in HR
- **Encourage work-life balance.** Model work-life balance yourself so staff feel permission to take care of themselves
- **Support time off.** Recognize burnout signs and help staff take recovery days
- **Promote peer support.** Build informal networks where staff can talk openly
- **Partner with behavioral health.** Bring in training and access to mental health resources
- **Celebrate staff.** Recognize hard work and effort, so staff feel valued

Wellness isn't "soft." It's a leadership responsibility **because you can't build a resilient team if your people are running on empty,** and investing in staff wellness will always pay back in morale, professionalism, safety, and outcomes.

Leadership's Ongoing Role in People Development

Building a professional workforce doesn't end when a hire clears probation. It's an ongoing leadership responsibility, one that requires attention, consistency, and presence.

One of the biggest mistakes I see in correctional leadership is **delegating all people development** "**down the line,**" handing off training to HR, letting supervisors "handle" new staff, and assuming good culture will just grow on its own. It won't.

Leadership drives culture, and culture lives in your people. That means the director, command staff, and frontline leaders must stay engaged in:

- who is hired
- how new staff are trained
- how expectations are reinforced
- how supervisors are coached
- how professionalism is modeled every day

You cannot lead culture from the sidelines. You have to stay in it, walking the floor, getting to know your people, and helping them grow. The staff you develop today will be the leadership team or the risk factor of tomorrow, depending on how you lead.

And the reality is that facilities that invest in people development every day see better outcomes in everything else, to include:

- Safer operations
- Healthier culture
- Better staff morale
- Improved partnerships
- Stronger public trust

When leadership owns this responsibility, when you make it clear that "building our people" is part of your daily job, culture grows stronger, and the facility becomes one the entire team can be proud of.

In the end, you don't just manage a jail. You lead people, too. And those people are the heart of everything your facility will become.

Reflection Questions

1. How intentional is your current hiring process? Are you hiring for professionalism and values?
2. What message are new hires receiving about culture both in training and from leadership presence?
3. How are you building leadership capacity at every level in your facility?
4. What steps are you taking to invest in staff wellness, and how can you do more?
5. How involved are you personally in shaping the development of your people, and how can you lead this work more effectively?

Chapter 7

SUSTAINING CULTURE THROUGH ACCOUNTABILITY AND CONSISTENCY

"What you allow is what will continue."

"What you tolerate is what you promote."
Crayman J. Harvey

I'll be honest—this chapter is one of the hardest to write because it is one of the hardest things to do in leadership: confront issues head-on when the culture needs it most.

Many leaders in corrections today find themselves in a place where they are not naturally confrontational or where they have learned to avoid conflict. Sometimes, however, the environment you inherit needs a face-to-face leader, someone willing to confront the issues that are killing the organization without hesitation.

To those leaders, I would say this: *Sir or Ma'am, your facility needs you to step up to confront what is harming your people, your culture, and your mission. Will it make you unpopular? Sometimes. Will you lose some people along the way? Yes. But think of it as a weeding process with you as the farmer clearing the flower bed because the good can't grow if the bad is choking it out.*

If you are serious about sustaining a healthy culture, about building the kind of facility that staff respect and the community can trust, you cannot avoid accountability.

And that starts with leadership showing the way.

Why Consistency Builds Trust

In corrections, **consistency is one of the most powerful leadership tools you have** and one of the easiest to lose. Why? Because people in this field don't just listen to what leaders say; they watch what leaders do. They watch for patterns. They pay attention to how leadership handles similar issues at different times, or with different people.

And if they see inconsistency—if one staff member is disciplined while another is ignored, if expectations change from shift to shift, or if accountability depends on who's involved—trust erodes fast. It doesn't matter how good your policies are, how strong your mission sounds, or how many inspirational talks you give. **If leadership consistency is weak, trust will be weak.**

I tell leadership teams this all the time: **Consistency is what turns good intentions into culture.** Without it, your best efforts won't stick, and the facility will slide toward cynicism, rumor, and disengagement. When leadership is consistent, in communication, in expectations, in accountability, staff trust grows. They know what is expected. They know where the line is. They know what will be tolerated and what won't. That clarity reduces stress, improves morale, and helps good staff do their best work.

When leadership is inconsistent, staff stop trusting. They become cynical. They start focusing on protecting themselves and not on doing their job well.

If you want to sustain a positive culture, **you must lead with consistency every day** because in this field, what you do every day matters more than what you say you'll do.

The Role of Accountability in Sustaining Culture

Accountability is the engine that sustains culture. It is how leadership signals every day what matters in the facility. **Without accountability, even good culture will erode and bad habits spread.** Why? Because staff watch closely:

- What does leadership tolerate?
- What happens when someone crosses the line?
- Are standards real or just words on paper?

If leadership is clear about expectations but fails to enforce them, the message is clear: *It's not really that important.* If leadership applies accountability to some but not to others, staff will disengage or worse, they will mirror the double standard.

What you tolerate is what you promote.

I remember a time when one of my lead supervisors mistakenly released an inmate in error. It was a serious issue made worse by the fact that this same supervisor had committed a similar infraction less than six months earlier. After careful review, the leadership team made the decision to demote her based on the repeated mistake.

During the counseling meeting, as her manager explained the reasoning behind the demotion, her first words were, "Why now? The first time this happened, no one said anything."

That response told me everything. The real problem wasn't just the error; it was that **inconsistent accountability in the past had left this supervisor confused about what would actually be tolerated.** In her mind, because the first mistake went unaddressed, the expectation wasn't clear. That lack of consistency had allowed bad habits to take root.

That's why consistent accountability is so critical:
- It reinforces values
- It protects professionalism
- It prevents the drift back to old habits
- It keeps staff morale healthy because fairness matters to staff

I often remind leadership teams that **staff can live with tough rules if they are fair, clear, and consistent. What they can't live with is unpredictability and favoritism.** Inconsistency in accountability damages trust faster than almost anything else.

If you want to sustain culture, the kind of culture you've worked hard to build, you must hold the line. And that starts with leadership modeling accountability first then applying it across the facility without exception. In this field, **leadership that fails to hold the line today will be forced to answer for it tomorrow.**

How Leadership Sets the Standard Every Day

Culture is not built in big events; it is built in daily moments. One of the biggest leadership myths in corrections is the idea that culture is something you can "announce" or "train once." It's not. **Culture is built and sustained by how leadership shows up every day.**

Modern Jail Leadership

Every conversation, every correction, every time you model professionalism or fail to shapes the tone of your facility. Staff are always watching leadership for cues. *Is this really important? Does leadership practice what they preach? Will they hold the line today or look the other way?*

I remind leadership teams that **micro-moments matter**. Culture is built on them.

- How you handle a disrespectful tone in briefing
- How you respond to staff gossip or negativity
- Whether you praise professional behavior when you see it
- Whether you follow through on a promise or let it slide

What happens when no one is watching—that's the real culture. And staff know. If leadership models accountability, professionalism, and respect every day, culture strengthens. If leadership looks the other way when "favorites" slip or allows small standards to erode, culture weakens fast.

This is why presence matters so much. The more leadership is seen on the floor—not just in an office—the more chances you have to shape these moments.

Building Supervisor Buy-in for Accountability

If you want to sustain culture, your frontline supervisors must be your strongest allies not your weakest link. **Middle leadership drives daily culture** more than any policy memo from the top. You can have the clearest expectations as a director, but if your corporals, sergeants, and lieutenants are inconsistent— if they avoid accountability, play favorites, or look the other way—the facility will follow their lead.

Staff watch their direct supervisors every day, and if they see supervisors enforcing expectations fairly and consistently, staff will align. But if they see supervisors tolerating poor behavior, even once, the message spreads fast that it's okay if they behave poorly, too.

That's why **building supervisor buy-in is one of the most important jobs of leadership.**

When asking for buy-in, I often use what I call the **Camelot Round Table Method.** I invite my core leadership team—command staff and those I directly supervise—and then I also invite one core member of their team to the table. This does two things: it breaks down barriers—frontline leaders feel heard and included, and it gives supervisors ownership because they help shape the message and direction, not just receive it.

I've seen great benefits from this approach: better communication, stronger accountability, and more consistent follow-through. When supervisors feel like they are part of the leadership vision and not just being "told what to do," buy-in increases dramatically. Beyond that, leadership must:

- **Coach supervisors early.** Don't assume because they've been promoted, they know

how to lead accountability. Teach it. Reinforce it.
- **Be clear on expectations.** Supervisors must understand that holding the line is part of your job; it's not optional.
- **Model it yourself.** If command staff avoids accountability or plays politics, supervisors will mirror it. Leadership must set the example.
- **Support supervisors when they do it right.** When a sergeant addresses an issue fairly, especially with a peer or a strong personality, back them up. That builds trust.
- **Correct drift quickly.** When you see supervisors tolerating poor behavior or avoiding hard conversations, step in fast because drift at that level spreads fast.
- **Supervisors are your culture drivers.** If they buy in, the culture gets stronger every day. If they don't, your best efforts will stall.

That's why leadership must invest time consistently building that buy-in because you can't build a professional facility without professional frontline leadership.

Managing Accountability for Senior Staff and Peers

One of the hardest but most important tests of leadership is how you handle accountability with your own peers and senior staff. It's easy to hold a new hire accountable. It's harder to hold a lieutenant, captain, or longtime staff member accountable, especially when relationships are close, history runs deep, or you know pushback will come. But here's the truth: **Staff watch how leadership holds leadership accountable.** If the frontline sees command staff or favored supervisors skating by on issues that others would be disciplined for, trust collapses fast.

I've seen it happen. Good officers lose trust in leadership not because of one policy, but because of inconsistency at the top. It sends the message "It depends who you are." And when that takes root, morale suffers, and cynicism spreads. **Leaders must model accountability even when it's hard.** Especially when it's hard. Here's what works:

- **Be clear. No one is above the standard.** Leadership must live it first.
- **Address issues quietly when appropriate but *do* address them.**
- **Don't play favorites because staff will see it.**
- **Back up your supervisors when they hold senior staff accountable or else they'll stop trying.**

- **Document and be transparent; fair processes protect everyone.**

I tell leadership teams that they will gain more respect holding one popular peer accountable than by disciplining ten new hires. Because when staff see leadership willing to "hold their own" to the standard, that's when trust grows. That's when people believe in the culture. And that is how you sustain accountability and culture in the long term.

The Connection Between Consistency and Morale

I've seen it in every facility I've worked in: **When leadership is consistent, morale improves. When leadership is inconsistent, morale crumbles.** It's really that simple.

Staff don't need leadership to be perfect, but they do need it to be fair, clear, and steady. In this field, where the work is already hard, the one thing that helps staff stay engaged is knowing what's expected and knowing leadership will be consistent in how those expectations are applied.

Inconsistent leadership does more damage to morale than almost anything else. I've seen it turn strong teams into divided, cynical groups in a matter of months. When one person gets away with what others are disciplined for, morale drops. When one shift is held accountable while another is ignored, morale drops. When policies change depending on who's on duty, morale drops.

But when leadership is consistent across shifts, ranks, and situations, staff know they can trust the system. And when they trust leadership, they take pride in their work.

Fair and visible leadership gives people something to rally around. It encourages teamwork. It builds professional pride. And it strengthens the very culture leadership is trying to sustain. Leadership can't separate accountability from morale. If you want a positive, professional environment, the accountability must be clear, fair, and consistent every day. That's how trust grows. That's how good people stay. That's how culture lasts.

Leading Through Leadership Turnover

In corrections, leadership turnover is inevitable. People promote, retire, move on, and with every change, the culture of the facility is tested. If culture depends too much on one person—the director, a strong captain, a veteran sergeant—then every leadership change brings risk. Standards drift, morale weakens, divisions emerge. Staff think, *We'll see how the new person handles it.* And old bad habits can come back fast. That's why one of the most important parts of sustaining culture is **building it bigger than any one person**. Your job as a leader is not just to run the facility well while you're there. It is to leave behind a professional culture that will continue after you're gone. That starts with:

- **Developing leaders at every level** so the culture is reinforced by many voices, not just yours
- **Embedding accountability into systems, not personalities** so expectations survive leadership changes
- **Documenting and communicating the "why" of your culture** so new leaders understand what works
- **Being transparent with staff about the long view** so they know professionalism is not tied to any one leader's style

I often remind leadership teams, If you leave tomorrow, what will survive? What will staff say still matters? Strong culture can and should outlast leadership turnover. If it doesn't, then we didn't really build culture; we just managed it for a while.

The real measure of leadership is not what happens while you're in the seat; it's what happens after you leave it.

Reflection Questions

1. Where are you most consistent in your leadership today, and where do you need to be more consistent?

2. How well does your accountability system support your culture, and where is it falling short?
3. Are your frontline supervisors fully bought in to accountability and consistency? If not, what steps can you take?
4. How do you personally model accountability with staff, with peers, and with senior leaders?

If you left tomorrow, what part of your leadership culture would survive and what would fade?

Chapter 8

LEADERSHIP BEYOND THE WALLS: PROFESSIONALISM, COMMUNITY, AND THE FUTURE

"Leadership is not about the next election, it's about the next generation."
Simon Sinek

"Leadership legacy isn't about titles. It's about the professional culture you help create."
Crayman J. Harvey

If there's one thing I hope leaders take from this book, it's this: **your leadership extends beyond the walls of your facility.** The tone you set, the culture you build, and the professionalism you model impact not only your staff and detainees but also the broader community you serve.

Too often in corrections, leaders focus only on what happens inside the walls, that is, the daily challenges of staffing, operations, incidents. And yes, those are critical. But the public's trust in your jail, the partnerships you build, and your influence on the future of this field all depend on leadership that reaches beyond the badge, beyond the facility, and into the wider community. As a correctional leader today, your responsibility is bigger than ever and so is your opportunity.

Why Leadership Extends Beyond the Jail

Whether we like it or not, in corrections, **the community sees your leadership every day.** Not just through press releases or audits, but through:

- How staff carry themselves off duty
- How detainees speak about their experience after release
- How other justice partners—courts, law enforcement, probation—talk about your facility
- How your agency responds in times of crisis

In today's world of 24/7 media and instant social platforms, the walls are not what they used to be. The public sees and judges your facility not by what you say, but by how you lead. That's why I believe leadership must extend well beyond the badge and beyond the booking door. It's our responsibility to:

- Set the tone for professionalism in how staff represent the agency
- Build trust with community partners
- Lead transparency and accountability
- Help shift public perceptions of the correctional field

Staff also take their cues from this. If leadership shows that "community doesn't matter," staff disengage. But when leadership models pride in the profession and respect for public trust, staff follow. Your jail is part of the community's justice system, not separate from it, and leadership must act that way every single day.

Setting the Standard for Professionalism

One of the biggest shifts corrections leaders must embrace is that our profession is not just about custody; it's about professionalism. If you want your facility to earn trust with staff, with the courts, with the public, leadership must model professional standards every day, and it starts with this question: **How do we carry ourselves in uniform, in court, in community spaces, on social media?**

Every interaction reflects on your facility's reputation:

- The language staff uses when speaking to detainees
- The tone used when testifying in court
- How staff engage with healthcare partners or social service agencies
- How officers interact with the public off duty
- What leadership models in their own behavior

What the community sees becomes the jail's reputation.

I've seen it happen both ways. When staff carry themselves with professionalism—they are respectful, competent, and steady courts respond better, partners collaborate more willingly, and public trust grows. When staff carry a "just a jail" mindset—they are dismissive, negative, disengaged—the entire justice system suffers, and the community narrative shifts quickly in the wrong direction. That's why leadership must set the standard, and they can do this by:

- Speaking with professionalism at all times
- Treating staff and partners with respect
- Addressing unprofessional conduct on and off duty
- Helping staff see themselves as ambassadors for the agency

Modern Jail Leadership

In this field, **you are always representing**, and professionalism, like culture, must be led from the top-down.

Building Partnerships in the Community

Corrections doesn't and can't operate in isolation. No matter how strong your internal culture is, **the success of your facility depends on the partnerships you build beyond the walls.** Many of the outcomes that matter most, such as safe transitions, reduced recidivism, and community trust, rely on collaboration. No jail can achieve those things alone, which is why an important part of modern corrections leadership is building relationships with:

- Courts—judges, prosecutors, public defenders
- Law enforcement—patrol, investigations, task forces
- Healthcare providers—medical, mental health, and substance use treatment
- Re-entry services—housing, employment, education
- Advocacy groups—who can become allies or critics
- The media—local and regional

When these partnerships are strong, good things happen. Detainees leave with more support and better chances of success. The public sees the jail as part of a solutions-based justice system. The facility gains allies during times of crisis or scrutiny. When leadership neglects these relationships and the jail walls go up figuratively as well as physically, the facility becomes isolated, and isolated facilities attract more criticism, distrust, and risk.

One practical way I've worked to build partnerships is by hosting **"meet and greet" sessions throughout the community**. During these local events, we talk openly about the jail, our successes, and our opportunities. Most of the community doesn't know what you or your people actually do, and in the absence of information, assumptions fill the void. Often, that means negative assumptions. Your voice—and your presence—can clear that up. If you don't tell your story before someone else does, the media, critics, or social media will shape your narrative for you. When you lead that conversation with honesty, transparency, and professionalism, you build trust, one partner at a time.

Community trust must be led, and partnerships must be grown on purpose. It takes time, consistency, and a willingness to listen, but it pays off for your agency, your staff, your detainees, and your community.

Preparing Staff for Leadership Beyond the Badge

If leadership ends at the badge, it's not leadership; it's just a title. One of our jobs as leaders is to help staff see themselves as **professionals**—not just correctional officers, deputies, or civilian staff—but as public servants whose conduct, voice, and influence extend into the community. Whether they realize it or not, staff represents the agency on duty and off. The public watches how they interact in court, at events, on social media. Every interaction helps shape the facility's reputation and community trust

That's why I believe **part of leadership development is preparing staff for leadership beyond the badge** and helping them understand that they are always representing the agency. Professionalism doesn't stop at the gate, the way you talk about your work matters in the community and online, and you can be a positive or negative force in this field, depending on how you lead yourself. When staff see themselves as professionals, when they take pride in being part of something bigger, morale grows, behavior improves, and trust builds both inside the facility and in the wider community.

It's also why I encourage leadership teams to:

- Coach staff on **professional identity** not just tactics
- Talk openly about how public perception works
- Reinforce that corrections is **part of the justice system** not apart from it
- Support staff in building leadership skills that carry beyond the walls

In doing so, your best staff will become ambassadors for this profession in the community, in other agencies, and for the next generation of leaders.

The Role of Leadership in Shaping the Future of Corrections

Corrections is changing, whether we want it to or not. The mental health crisis, staffing challenges, shifts in public expectations, legal reforms—the field is evolving, and leadership must evolve with it. The worst thing we can do is lead by looking backward, trying to drag today's realities through an outdated lens. What worked twenty years ago won't meet today's challenges or tomorrow's.

That's why I believe leadership in corrections today must do more than just manage the present. It must also help shape the future of the profession. That means staying current and helping our teams do the same:

- Understanding mental health trends and how they impact custody
- Partnering with healthcare and re-entry providers in meaningful ways
- Building professional pride in a modern, ethical, transparent field
- Developing leadership at every level because the next generation needs mentors

- Staying connected to professional networks—AJA, NCCHC, ACA, and others—so we keep learning and leading
- Listening to staff, to the community, to the changing justice landscape

Because here's the truth: **if we don't shape the future of corrections, someone else will.** Courts, advocates, legislatures—all are stepping into this space, and if leadership is not at the table, leading with professionalism and vision, we'll be reacting to change instead of helping drive it.

I often tell my leadership teams that we are not just leading for today. We are building the future for this facility, for our staff, and for the field. The future of corrections is being written, and leadership must help write the best version of that story.

Leaving a Leadership Legacy

Every leader leaves a legacy, whether they intend to or not. The real question is **what kind of legacy will it be?**

When I talk with leadership teams, I often ask, "If you left this facility tomorrow, what would remain? What would staff say mattered here, and what would fade?" The truth is your policies may change, your programs may be revised, but the culture you build for better or worse will echo long after you move on.

Leadership legacy isn't about titles. It isn't about awards. It's about the professional culture you help create.

- Did you build trust?
- Did you raise expectations?
- Did you invest in your people?
- Did you model professionalism on and off duty?
- Did you help grow leaders for the next generation?

A facility with a strong, professional culture can weather leadership transitions, legal challenges, and media storms, but a facility that leans too heavily on one personality or tolerates old habits will drift fast the moment leadership changes.

That's why I believe one of the most important parts of leadership is **growing other leaders**—passing the torch, not just carrying it. Invest in your staff, your supervisors, your future captains so that the culture survives you. In this profession, as in any, **we are all temporary stewards**. The question is: *What will you leave behind? Will the facility, the team, and the profession be stronger because you were there?*

That is leadership legacy. And that is what we should all strive to build.

Reflection Questions

1. How are you leading professionalism—not just custody—in your facility today?
2. What partnerships could you strengthen to improve outcomes for staff, detainees, and the community?
3. How are you helping staff see themselves as professionals, both on and off duty?
4. How are you preparing your team for the future of corrections not just today's challenges?
5. What leadership legacy do you want to leave, and what steps are you taking to build it now?

Closing Thoughts

Leadership in corrections is not easy work. It never has been, and in today's environment, the challenges are greater than ever. However, it is some of the most important leadership there is because what happens inside our jails affects real lives, not just for those in custody, but for staff, for families, and for the community.

Every day, as a leader, you shape that reality. Through your tone. Through your consistency. Through how you develop your people. Through how you build trust beyond the walls. Through how you leave the facility better than you found it.

If there is one thing I hope you take from this book, it is this: **leadership is not about control—it's about influence.** It's about setting the example, building the culture, and investing in people so that long after your watch is done, the facility continues to grow stronger.

I've had the privilege and sometimes the pain of leading through crisis, change, and rebuilding, and if I've learned one truth, it is this: **Culture survives leadership change if you build it well.**

So build well, lead with purpose, and help move this profession forward for your staff, for your facility, and for the communities we all serve.

References & Resources

American Jail Association (AJA). Articles, leadership resources, and professional publications.

Harvey, Crayman J. (May/June 2025). "Security Is the Foundation, But Not the House: Addressing Healthcare and Rehabilitation in U.S. Jails." *American Jails* magazine.

Knapp, Diana, MS, CCE, CJM. Director of Corrections, Jackson County Detention Center (Kansas City, Missouri). 1st Vice President of the American Jail Association. Chair of AJA's Corrections Leadership Committee. Leadership presentations and professional publications.

National Commission on Correctional Health Care (NCCHC). Standards, guidelines, and leadership resources.

National Institute for Jail Operations (NIJO). Training materials and leadership publications.

Sinek, S. (2014). *Leaders Eat Last: Why Some Teams Pull Together and Other's Don't.* Penguin Publishing.

Syrus, Publilius. Quoted leadership wisdom.

U.S. Department of Justice (DOJ). 2025. "Findings Report on the Alvin S. Glenn Detention Center."

Ziglar, Z. (2000). *See You at the Top.* Pelican Publishing.

ABOUT THE AUTHOR

Crayman J. Harvey is a veteran correctional leader, consultant, educator, and speaker with more than 20 years of experience across law enforcement, adult and juvenile corrections, and facility leadership.

He is the former director of Alvin S. Glenn Detention Center (Richland County, SC), where he led major reform efforts during a period of federal investigation and operational crisis. He currently serves as director of the Kershaw County Detention Center and is the founder of Harvey Consulting LLC, where he advises agencies nationwide on correctional leadership, healthcare reform, compliance, and building professional facility culture.

Harvey has extensive leadership experience across both juvenile justice and adult corrections and previously led a state juvenile facility in South Carolina. In addition to operational leadership, he has served as an adjunct professor of criminal justice at Central

Carolina Technical College, helping educate and mentor the next generation of justice professionals.

He holds certifications as a Certified Jail Manager (CJM), Certified Correctional Health Professional (CCHP), and Lean Six Sigma Green Belt from the University of South Carolina. His academic achievements include a Bachelor of Arts in Psychology from Saint Leo University, a Master of Arts in Administration of Justice from the University of Phoenix, and a Master Certificate in High-Performance Leadership from the National Association of Counties (NACo).

Mr. Harvey is also certified as a Class 1 and Class 2 law enforcement officer and serves as a field training officer.

He is an active member of the American Jail Association (AJA), the National Commission on Correctional Health Care (NCCHC), and the American Correctional Association (ACA).

A passionate advocate for modern, professional corrections, Harvey speaks regularly at national and regional leadership conferences, correctional summits, and professional training events.

www.ingramcontent.com/pod-product-compliance
Lightning Source LLC
Chambersburg PA
CBHW071222160426
43196CB00012B/2388